THE ARTIST'S JOURNEY

ALSO BY STEVEN PRESSFIELD

FICTION

The Legend of Bagger Vance
Gates of Fire
Tides of War
Last of the Amazons
The Virtues of War
The Afghan Campaign
Killing Rommel
The Profession
The Knowledge
36 Righteous Men (2019)

NONFICTION

The War of Art
The Warrior Ethos
Turning Pro
The Authentic Swing
Do the Work
The Lion's Gate
An American Jew
Nobody Wants to Read Your Sh*t

THE ARTIST'S JOURNEY

THE WAKE OF
THE HERO'S JOURNEY AND
THE LIFELONG PURSUIT OF MEANING

STEVEN PRESSFIELD

Black Irish Entertainment LLC

BLACK IRISH ENTERTAINMENT LLC
223 EGREMONT PLAIN ROAD
PMB 191
EGREMONT, MA 01230

FIRST BLACK IRISH ENTERTAINMENT PAPERBACK EDITION JULY 2018

FOR INFORMATION ABOUT SPECIAL DISCOUNTS FOR BULK PURCHASES,
PLEASE VISIT WWW.BLACKIRISHBOOKS.COM

ISBN: 978-1-936891-54-2
EBOOK: 978-1-936891-56-6

For T. R. Goodman,
who has propelled me powerfully
along my own artist's journey.

THE ARTIST'S JOURNEY

I found that what I had desired all my life was not to live—if what others are doing is called living—but to express myself. I realized that I had never had the least interest in living, but only in this which I am doing now, something which is parallel to life, of it at the same time, and beyond it. What is true interests me scarcely at all, nor even what is real; only that interests me which I imagine to be, that which I had stifled every day in order to live.

Henry Miller
Tropic of Capricorn

DARK NIGHT OF THE SOUL

At least once a day (sometimes three or four), someone sends me an e-mail describing, with excruciating vividness, their losing struggle with their own Resistance. Many of these letters are heartbreaking. They plead for help. "How," they ask, "can I stop drinking/doing drugs/self-destructing/beating my spouse/ neglecting my children and start doing my best work/my soul's desire? How can I keep up my will to fight?"

In Hollywood terms, we would say of these writers that they are at their All Is Lost moment.

They are at that point in their hero's journey where they are as far from their objective as possible.

They are torn between their *daimon*—the inhering spirit summoning them to live out their higher destiny—and the very real demands and fears of the material world in which they (and their families) dwell.

MY OWN ALL IS LOST MOMENT

I'm twenty-four years old, married, and working as an advertising writer in New York City, at an agency called Benton & Bowles.

Stuck in the Boring World.

I've got a boss named Ed Hannibal. He quits and writes a novel. It's a huge success. I think, "Hell, why don't I do the same thing?"

The Call.

I do quit. I've got a wife I love. She supports me. I start writing.

I'm trying to write a novel. I have no idea what a novel is, or what writing is. And I certainly have no idea what Resistance is.

The Villain appears.

Short version: I get 99.9% of the way through and I freak out. I blow up the book and my marriage. Shorter version: I wind up on the American road in my '65 Chevy van.

Act Two. The Upside-Down World.

I cross the US thirteen times, working all the jobs a screwed-up writer works. I teach school. I pick fruit. I drive trucks. I work on offshore oil rigs.

Archetypes appear.

I meet and become friends with older mentors, helpful and non-helpful women. Even spirit animals.

The ordeal deepens.

I'm fighting my own cowardice in running away from writing, plus my guilt over hurting my wife, disgracing my family, etc. In total defeat, I crawl back to New York City and find work driving a cab. What's left for me? I can't go back out on the road, and I can't find my way forward.

I have hit my own All Is Lost moment.

THE EPIPHANAL MOMENT

In Hollywood parlance, the All Is Lost moment is succeeded, often immediately, by the Epiphanal Moment.

In this moment, the hero experiences a breakthrough.

This breakthrough is almost always internal. The hero changes her attitude. She regroups. She sees her dilemma from a new perspective—one that she had never considered before (or, if she had considered it, had rejected)—a point of view that offers either hope or desperation amounting to hope.

The narrative now enters Act Three. The hero, fortified by this fresh hope (or desperation), charges full-tilt into the climax.

Sarah Connor stops running and turns to confront the Terminator.

Luke Skywalker boards his X-wing and flies against the Death Star.

Bogey makes the decision to put Ingrid, with her husband Paul, onto the plane to Lisbon, while he himself stays to confront the enemies of freedom.

Here's my Epiphanal Moment, as described in *The War of Art*:

> I washed up in New York a couple of decades ago, making twenty bucks a night driving a cab and running away full-time from doing my work. One night, alone in my $110-a

month sublet, I hit bottom in terms of having diverted myself into so many phony channels so many times that I couldn't rationalize it for one more evening. I dragged out my ancient Smith Corona, dreading the experience as pointless, fruitless, meaningless, not to say the most painful exercise I could think of. For two hours I made myself sit there, torturing out some trash that I chucked immediately into the shitcan. That was enough. I put the machine away. I went back to the kitchen. In the sink sat ten days of dishes. For some reason I had enough excess energy that I decided to wash them. The warm water felt pretty good. The soap and sponge were doing their thing. A pile of clean plates began rising in the drying rack. To my amazement I realized I was whistling.

It hit me that I had turned a corner.

I was okay.

I would be okay from here on.

Do you understand? I hadn't written anything good. It might be years before I would, if I ever did at all. That didn't matter. What counted was that I had, after years of running from it, actually sat down and done my work.

This was my epiphanal moment.

My hero's journey was over.

My artist's journey had begun.

BOOK ONE

OUT OF THE DARKNESS
The Wake of the Hero's Journey

THE HERO'S JOURNEY

The hero's journey is a myth that, according to Joseph Campbell, C. G. Jung and others, is common to all human cultures. This template exists in our psyches from birth, like an operating system or, perhaps more exactly, a piece of software within the operating system.

Here's a cheat sheet to the hero's journey, with a tip o' the hat appreciation to Joseph Campbell (*The Hero with a Thousand Faces*), Christopher Vogler (*The Writer's Journey*), and Blake Snyder (*Save the Cat!*).

The stages of the hero's journey (roughly) are:

1. THE ORDINARY WORLD
    The hero, i.e., you or me or Dorothy or Rocky or Luke Skywalker, is introduced in his or her regular, normal world. But beneath the surface, powerful currents of change and transformation are already in motion ...

2. THE CALL
    Some outside event (or it could be internal) breaks in on the hero, alerting or even compelling her or him to take action and leave the Ordinary World behind.

3. REFUSAL OF THE CALL

The hero always balks, at least for a moment. Rocky turns down the chance to fight the champ, Odysseus feigns insanity to get out of going to the Trojan War.

4. THE MENTOR APPEARS

Hello, Obi-Wan Kenobi! Or the mentor may arise internally, in a dream or a vision. The hero is infused with courage and overcomes his or her fear of launching into the unknown.

5. CROSSING THE THRESHOLD

Hero says goodbye to the familiar, sets out into the Extraordinary World (or, in Blake Snyder's very apt term, the Inverted World.) Dorothy leaves Kansas, Conan the Barbarian sets out from the Wheel of Pain.

6. TRIALS AND TRIBULATIONS, FRIENDS AND FOES

Huck and Jim fend off rednecks, crackers, peckerwoods, mob attacks, not to mention the king and the duke. The Inverted World tests our heroes, but sends allies and teachers as well.

7. PRIMAL ORDEAL

The hero enters the Lair of Evil, comes face to face with her "heart of darkness." Theseus confronts the Minotaur in the belly of the Labyrinth, Indiana Jones goes after the golden statue, Bogey makes his all-or-nothing play for Ingrid ...

8. THE PAYOFF
    Hero succeeds! But wait ...

9. GETTING OUT
    Bad Guys rally. They cannot let Jason get home with the Golden Fleece! Indy flees. Dorothy bolts. Odysseus escapes Circe (not to mention the Cyclops, Scylla and Charybdis, etc.) and sails for home.

10. RESURRECTION
    One final, hellacious test. The hero, in Christopher Vogler's phrase, "is purified by a last sacrifice," achieves a moment of rebirth in which the initial internal issue that was tormenting her is at last resolved.

11. A GIFT FOR THE PEOPLE
    The hero returns to the place from which he originally set forth. But he does not come home empty-handed. He brings a transforming wisdom, an "elixir," that he donates to the wider community, to save it and bring it peace.

THE HERO'S JOURNEY AND
THE ARTIST'S JOURNEY

I have a theory about the Hero's Journey. We all have one. We have many, in fact. But our primary hero's journey as artists is the passage we live out, in real life, *before* we find our calling.

The hero's journey is the search for that calling.

It's preparation.

It's initiation (or, more precisely, self-initiation).

On our hero's journey, we see, we experience, we suffer. We learn.

On our hero's journey, we acquire a history that is ours alone. It's a secret history, a private history, a personal history. No one has it but us. No one knows it but us. This secret history is the most valuable possession we hold, or ever will hold. We will draw upon it for the rest of our lives.

The hero's journey ends when, like Odysseus, we return home to Ithaca, to the place from which we started. We wash up on shore. We have survived. We have come home.

Now what?

The passage that comes next is the Artist's Journey.

The artist's journey comes *after* the hero's journey.

Everything that has happened to us up to this point is rehearsal for us to act, now, as our true self and to find and speak in our true voice.

The artist's journey is the process of self-discovery that follows.

It will last as long as we're alive, and maybe longer.

THE HERO'S JOURNEY
IS A LIVING, BREATHING THING

There are two aspects to the hero's journey—by which I mean the template that exists from birth in our psyches—that are, in my view, often overlooked or not taken into account.

1.   The template is a fill-in-the-blanks proposition. It lays out a pattern and a sequence but it leaves the details specific to the individual TK (to come).

2.   The hero's journey template exerts a powerful, almost irresistible pressure on the individual to *live it out in real life.*

As a young childless woman experiences the ticking of her biological clock, so you and I feel the pull of our as-yet-unlived hero's journey.

What makes us leave our small town and head to the big city? Why do we enlist in the Special Forces? What is happening beneath the surface when we meet a stranger on a plane and follow her (or him) to Argentina?

The hero's journey software in our heads is demanding to be lived out.

The blanks are insisting on being filled in.

The hero (_____) receives the Call when (_____) walks into his/her life and does/says (_____).

Hero crosses the Threshold of Adventure at (_____) place and (_____) time. He/she encounters Monsters (_____) and (_____) and is assisted by Allies (_____) and (_____).

The hero returns safely at last to (_____), the place from which she/he started, by means of a (_____), bringing for the people the gift of (_____), hard-won from his/her experiences.

If you're an artist, I can fill in the final blank for you right now.

The gift you bring is the works you will produce.

THE CONTENTS OF
OUR HERO'S JOURNEY

My own hero's journey lasted about two and a half years—from age twenty-six to twenty-nine. It hit every beat in the myth, by the numbers and in sequence.

I had no idea, of course, that what I was experiencing might be called a hero's journey. I had never heard of the hero's journey.

What was clear to me was that *something* was happening, and that something was a train I couldn't stop or slow down or get off.

What was clear too was when it ended. I knew the exact moment. I could feel it.

Even then, in that hour, I understood that the experience was of supreme value and importance. I didn't need hindsight. I knew in the moment.

My family may have been repelled, even appalled by where I had been and what I had done; my friends may have feared for my sanity; others who cared for me may have shaken their heads at the waste and folly and futility. Even I understood it would take me years to recover. I didn't care. The trip was worth it.

Why?

Because I now had a history that was mine alone. I had an ordeal that I had survived and a passage that I had paid for with my own blood. Nobody knew about this passage but me. Nobody would ever know, nor did I feel the slightest urge to communicate it. This was mine, and nobody could ever take it away from me.

I had punched my ticket.

I had filled in the blanks.

A GIFT FOR THE PEOPLE

In the mythology of the hero's journey, the hero at the conclusion of her ordeal returns home safely from her wanderings. But she does not arrive empty-handed. She returns with an "elixir," a "gift for the people."

This gift is the product of the hero's solitary suffering. It may be wisdom or queenly command. It may come with fire or the sword, driving out the evil forces that have infested the kingdom. Or it may come gently, as poetry or music that heals and restores harmony to the land.

You, the seeker, have at last returned home.

You are an artist now, as you have always wished to be.

What gift do you bring for the people?

You will learn that, now, on your artist's journey.

WHAT IS AN ARTIST?

Before we dig deeper into the nature of the artist's journey, let's pause for a moment and ask ourselves, "What exactly *is* an artist?

What qualities can we attribute to this peculiar subspecies of the human race?

AN ARTIST HAS A SUBJECT

Mean Streets
Taxi Driver
The Last Waltz
Raging Bull
Goodfellas
Cape Fear
Casino
Gangs of New York
The Aviator
The Departed
Hugo
Shutter Island
The Wolf of Wall Street
Silence

Did Martin Scorsese sit down as a young filmmaker and ask himself, "What's my subject?" I doubt it very much.

But a subject arose just the same. (Actually probably two: Outlaw Life and Love of Cinema, with a couple of outliers thrown in.)

You have a subject too.

You were born with it.

You will discover it on your artist's journey.

WHAT IS "SUBJECT"?

Subject does not mean "the Civil War" or "feminism."

Consider Bruce Springsteen's subject. It isn't just dudes and babes in cars in New Jersey.

It's thematic. The Boss's theme, to which he returns over and over, is the worth of passion and the integrity of what we might call "the common man" (and woman).

His subject is red-white-and-blue, fucked-over, fucked-up, but still shining and worthy and unbreakable.

Subject is deeper than topic. It's not "what it's about," it's what it's *really* about.

HOW SUBJECT ARISES

It sounds facile to say, "We don't pick our subject. Our subject picks us." But I'm convinced that statement is true.

It's not *your* subject. It's your Self's, your Muse's, your Superconscious's.

You were born with that subject but you never knew it.

Have you ever met someone who says, "I have no passion for anything. I wish I could feel it, but I can't. The only thing I feel is boredom."

Bullshit.

I know this is a lie because I've lived it myself for years.

Show me someone who claims he doesn't give a shit and I'll show you a born artist who's scared out of his wits to become that artist.

Our subject is sitting right in front of us but we can't see it because we're terrified.

We're terrified that, if we recognize and acknowledge our subject (which is our calling as an artist), we'll have to act on it.

We'll have to make a decision.

We'll have to put ourselves on the line.

We'll have to take a risk.

I can say truthfully of every book I've written that, before I saw it as a subject, I had no idea I was even interested in it.

In fact I *wasn't* interested in it. Or if I was, I dismissed that interest as purely idiosyncratic—a feeling that applied to me only but would never apply to anyone else.

The books picked me. I didn't pick them.

It's a mystery, this art racket.

MY SUBJECT

The Legend of Bagger Vance
Gates of Fire
Tides of War
Last of the Amazons
The Virtues of War
The War of Art
The Afghan Campaign
Killing Rommel
The Profession
Do The Work
Turning Pro
The Warrior Ethos
The Authentic Swing
The Lion's Gate
An American Jew
The Knowledge
Nobody Wants to Read Your Sh*t
36 Righteous Men

Even if you haven't read any of these books, you can tell just from the titles that they possess a unified subject.

Three critical points:

One, this subject materialized *on its own*. There was no plan on my part. No conscious decision. No moment of inflection.

Two, the subject was an absolute surprise to me. It revealed itself book by book, year by year, obsession by obsession.

Three, I had no choice as an artist except to follow this subject, and serve it, as it revealed itself and evolved over time.

AN ARTIST HAS A VOICE

The Deer Hunter
Sophie's Choice
Kramer vs. Kramer
Silkwood
Julia
Out of Africa
Ironweed
Heartburn
The Bridges of Madison County
Doubt
A Cry in the Dark
Postcards from the Edge
Adaptation
The Devil Wears Prada
The Iron Lady
Into the Woods
Ricki and the Flash
The Post

A Meryl Streep performance is as recognizably Streepian as a song by Jackson Browne is Browneian or a dance program by Twyla Tharp is Tharpian.

Did these artists get lucky? Were they born with voices? Or did they find and acquire them on their artists' journeys?

AN ARTIST HAS A
MEDIUM OF EXPRESSION

For Stephen King, it was fantasy/horror, which evolved over time into more ambitious and literary forms. For Bob Dylan, it was folk music, which likewise developed into higher and more innovative idioms.

A critical part of the artist's journey is answering the question, "What is my medium of expression?"

AN ARTIST HAS A POINT OF VIEW

When I first started working on movie sets, I used to marvel at how the director could answer so many questions from so many people so quickly and with such authority. "Where do you want the camera?" "What mark should the actress hit?" "How long till lunch?"

"There."

"There."

"Forty minutes."

How did the director do it? How did he always know?

One day I asked.

"Because," the director answered, "I have a point of view."

In other words, the director *knew what movie he was making.*

He knew what it was about (subject).

He knew what he wanted it to look and sound like (voice, medium of expression, and style).

PICASSO HAD A POINT OF VIEW

When Georges Braque and the early Cubists first painted portraits that had two eyes on one side of a woman's face, critics were outraged. Art lovers were appalled. Intellectuals were brawling with each other in bistros in Montmartre and Saint-Germain-des-Prés.

But Braque knew. Picasso knew. Leger knew.

They had a point of view.

The Cubists could draw a representational face. But that wasn't what they wanted. That wasn't their point of view.

Caesar had a point of view.

Gandhi had a point of view.

Martin Luther King, Jr. had a point of view.

The artist can answer any question (including those posed by herself) when she has a point of view.

AN ARTIST HAS A STYLE

Picasso didn't paint those crazy Cubist faces because it was the only way he knew how to draw. Nor did Hemingway employ short words because he couldn't spell antidisestablishmentarianism.

Style is inseparable from voice. It evolves out of subject and point of view and blends seamlessly with medium of expression.

The artist on her journey may try out a number of styles before finding her own.

Each one of these—subject, voice, point of view, medium of expression, and style—is an aspect of the single question, "What is my gift?" which is itself another way of asking, "Who am I?"

AN ARTIST IS IN TOUCH
WITH HER TIME

By "time," I mean era or generation. Picasso's Cubism and Hemingway's equally multi-planed prose both evolved out of the mass-mechanical, herky-jerky style and rhythm of the era before and after World War I (a period that also produced the machine gun and the self-amortizing mortgage). So did Gershwin's *Rhapsody in Blue* and Robert Johnson's *Love in Vain* and, a little later, Henry Miller's *Tropic of Capricorn*.

All were responses to the times these artists lived in.

If we want to get mysto on this subject (and I always do) we could say that the souls of these writers, painters, and musicians chose the epoch they wished to be born into, for reasons that the artists themselves possibly never knew or even inquired about.

Even artists whose works seem to be out of their own time—flashing backward, Gore Vidal with *Burr* or *Lincoln* or, forward, anything by Philip K. Dick—are, if you look closely enough, burrowed deeply into the zeitgeist, only from a different temporal angle.

The artist in her journey speaks to and of her time.

THE ORDINARY WORLD
AND THE EXTRAORDINARY WORLD

We said that the artist has a subject, a voice, a point of view, a medium of expression, and a style.

But where do these come from?

How do we find our own?

In my experience the process is neither rational nor logical. It can't be commanded. It can't be rushed. It is not subject to the will or the ego.

We are born, I believe, with everything we are seeking—a subject, a voice, a point of view, a medium of expression, and a style. But these reside in an area of the psyche outside the range of conventional consciousness.

The artist's journey is a parallel to the hero's journey in that you and I, the artists-in-embryo, must leave our Ordinary World (the conscious mind) and cross the threshold into the Extraordinary World (the unconscious or superconscious) to find and acquire our golden fleece (the knowledge of, and access to, our gift).

The process, like the hero's journey, involves time.

It involves suffering.

It involves folly.

Its crisis takes the form of an All Is Lost moment.

Once you have given up the ghost [wrote Henry Miller], *everything follows with dead certainty, even in the midst of chaos.*

The ghost that we give up is the ego. The illusion of control.

The "everything" that follows is our artist's power—our subject, our voice, our point of view, our medium of expression, and our style.

THE SHAPE OF
THE ARTIST'S JOURNEY

Consider the course and contour of this artist's journey:

Greetings from Asbury Park, N.J.
The Wild, the Innocent & the E Street Shuffle
Born to Run
Darkness on the Edge of Town
The River
Nebraska
Born in the USA
Tunnel of Love
Human Touch
Lucky Town
The Ghost of Tom Joad
Working on a Dream
Wrecking Ball
High Hopes
Springsteen on Broadway

Or this artist's:

Goodbye, Columbus
Portnoy's Complaint
The Great American Novel

My Life as a Man
The Professor of Desire
Zuckerman Unbound
The Anatomy Lesson
The Counterlife
Sabbath's Theater
American Pastoral
The Human Stain
The Plot Against America
Indignation
Nemesis

Or this artist's:

Clouds
Ladies of the Canyon
Blue
For the Roses
Court and Spark
The Hissing of Summer Lawns
Hejira
Don Juan's Reckless Daughter
Wild Things Run Fast
Chalk Mark in a Rain Storm
Night Ride Home
Turbulent Indigo

Clearly there is a unity (of subject, of theme, of voice, of style, of intention) to each of these writers' bodies of work.

There's a progression too, isn't there? The works, considered in sequence, feel like a journey that is advancing and evolving in a specific direction.

Bob Dylan
The Freewheelin' Bob Dylan
The Times They Are a-Changin'
Highway 61 Revisited
Blonde on Blonde
Bringing It All Back Home
Blood on the Tracks
Desire
John Wesley Harding
Street-Legal
Nashville Skyline
Slow Train Coming
Hard Rain
Time Out of Mind
Tempest
Shadows in the Night

You too possess an artist's journey.

Even if you have never yet written a song or completed a short story, that body of work lies dormant inside you.

It is percolating. It is exerting pressure—whether you feel it or not, whether you believe it or not.

Like the hero's journey, the artist's journey demands to be lived out. It demands to be expressed.

WHAT IS THE ARTIST'S JOURNEY?

The thesis of this book is that the artist's journey, which follows the hero's journey chronologically, comprises the true work, the actual production, of the artist's life.

From that moment, the epiphanal moment, the hero is no longer a free-range individual.

She has become an artist.

As Rosanne Cash declared in her extraordinary memoir, *Composed:*

> *I had awakened from the morphine sleep of success into the life of an artist.*

Everything in her life that is not-artist now falls away.

On the surface her new life may look ordinary, even boring. No more catastrophic romances. No more self-destructive binges. (Okay, maybe a few.) No more squandering or disrespecting her gift, her voice, her talent.

The artist is on a mission now.

Her life has acquired a purpose.

What is the artist's life about now?

It's about following her Muse.

It's about finding her voice.

It's about becoming who she really is.

On her journey, the artist will produce the works she was born to bring into being.

She will be on that journey for the rest of her life.

What, then, are the characteristics of the artist's journey?

THE ARTIST'S JOURNEY IS INTERNAL

I used to write at a desk that faced a wall. My friends would ask, "Why don't you turn the desk around so you have a view outside?"

I don't care about the view outside.

My focus is interior.

The book or movie I'm writing is playing *inside my head*.

Dalton Trumbo wrote in the bathtub.

Marcel Proust never got out of bed.

Why should they?

The journey they were on was inside themselves.

THE ARTIST'S JOURNEY IS PERSONAL

The novels of Philip Roth are completely different from those of Jonathan Franzen.

Neither author, gifted as he may be, can do what the other does.

In fact, neither can write anything at all except what his own gift authorizes, that which is unique to him alone.

THE ARTIST'S JOURNEY IS UNIVERSAL

And yet millions of people can read Philip Roth and Jonathan Franzen and be touched and moved and illuminated.

What is personal to the artist is universal to the rest of us.

THE ARTIST'S JOURNEY IS SOLITARY

Yes, artists collaborate. And yeah, there is such a thing as "the writers' room."

But the work of the artist takes place not on the page or in conversation or debate, but inside her head.

You, the artist, are alone in that space.

There is no one in there but you.

THE ARTIST'S JOURNEY IS MENTAL

The sculptor may shape marble or manipulate bronze. The architect may work in steel and stone. But these materials are merely the physical medium by which the artist expresses what she sees inside her mind.

The artist's real medium is thought.

Her product is the fruit of the imagination.

THE ARTIST'S JOURNEY IS AN EVOLUTION

We set forth as artists, you and I, from a Portsmouth of the mind and sail for an imaginary Indies. Storms arise along the way. We encounter monsters (and allies as well). Growth occurs. Progress is recorded.

The artist changes on this journey.

She is not the person at the end that she was at the beginning.

THE ARTIST'S JOURNEY IS A CONSTANT

And yet, no matter how profoundly or dramatically the artist's work evolves over her lifetime, her subject remains the same.

She may dive into it more deeply. She may come at it from wildly different directions. But her obsession remains unaltered throughout her life.

THE ARTIST'S JOURNEY IS
ABOUT SELF-DISCOVERY

I've read many times that art is self-expression. I don't believe it.

I don't believe the artist knows what he or she wishes to express.

The artist is being driven from a far deeper and more primal source than the conscious intellect. It is not an overstatement, in my view, to declare that the artist has no idea what he's doing.

As Socrates famously declared in Plato's *Phaedrus*:

> ... if a man comes to the door of poetry untouched by the madness of the Muses, believing that technique alone will make him a good poet, he and his sane compositions never reach perfection, but are utterly eclipsed by the performances of the inspired madman.

The artist is not expressing himself. He is *discovering* himself.

THE ARTIST'S JOURNEY IS
ABOUT THE ART, NOT THE ARTIST

Whom exactly is the artist discovering?

Is Dostoyevsky discovering Dostoyevsky?

Which Dostoyevsky?

Is Dostoyevsky discovering "Dostoyevsky"?

Or is "Dostoyevsky" discovering Dostoyevsky?

My answer is #4.

The artificial ego-entity that the world (and Dostoyevsky himself perhaps) believes to be Dostoyevsky is discovering a deeper, wider, smarter, braver personage that has traveled across leagues and eons to reach this present moment and will continue its passage long after "Dostoyevsky" is gone.

The artist himself is disposable.

What endures is the Self he is seeking, which is not "himself" but himself.

THE ARTIST'S JOURNEY IS DANGEROUS

The artist, like the mystic and the renunciant, does her work within an altered sphere of consciousness.

Seeking herself, her voice, her source, she enters the dark forest. She is alone. No friend or lover knows where her path has taken her.

Rules are different within this wilderness. Hatters are mad and principles inverted.

The artist has entered this sphere of her own free will. She has deliberately unmoored herself from conventional consciousness. This is her calling. This is what she was born to do.

Will she come out safely?

ON THE ARTIST'S JOURNEY, ALL ENEMIES ARE MENTAL

Fear of failure.

Fear of success.

Fear of the new, of pain, of loneliness, of exertion, of intensity.

Need for external (third-party) validation.

Self-doubt.

Arrogance.

Impatience.

Inability to defer gratification.

Predisposition to distraction.

Shallowness of thought and purpose.

Conventionality.

Insularity.

The need to cling to the known.

None of these enemies is real in the sense that, say, a lion is real, or a man with a gun.

All are products of the mind.

ON THE ARTIST'S JOURNEY, ALL ENEMIES ARE SELF-GENERATED

The artist on her journey confronts no foes that are not of her own creation.

Her fear is her own. Her vanity. Her need for adulation, for the attention of others, for titillation, for distraction.

Like Walter Pidgeon dueling the monsters of the Id in *Forbidden Planet*, the artist possesses within herself the capacity to overcome these enemies.

She has created them mentally.

She can defeat them the same way.

ON THE ARTIST'S JOURNEY, ALL STRENGTHS ARE MENTAL

Courage.

Honesty, particularly with oneself.

Self-confidence.

Humility.

Compassion for oneself and others.

The ability to receive criticism objectively.

Patience.

Curiosity, open-mindedness, receptivity to the new.

The ability to focus.

The ability to defer gratification.

Will.

Mental toughness.

The capacity to endure adversity, injustice, indifference.

ON THE ARTIST'S JOURNEY,
ALL STRENGTHS ARE SELF-GENERATED

None of the capacities listed in the previous chapter is innate, but all may be acquired by effort and force of will.

THE ARTIST'S JOURNEY IS
A JOURNEY OF THE IMAGINATION

I'm an American, and Americans have scant patience for anything that can't be reduced to a number (a sports score, say, or a sales figure). We Yanks feel comfortable in a world that can be cut and measured, boxed and shipped, extracted from the earth and hauled to market.

The artist's journey has nothing to do with that.

The artist on her journey will make everything up, including herself.

Her creations will be fictional, apparitional, chimerical. And yet the artist is neither a fabulist nor a charlatan. She is not lying. She is not deceiving.

Rather she sees, with the vision of imagination, what lies beneath the box scores and the market quotes.

She sees what is real and brings it forth so that others can see it.

THE ARTIST'S JOURNEY
IS A JOURNEY OF DREAMS

I never wrote anything good until I stopped trying to write the truth. I never had any real fun either.

Truth is not the truth.

Fiction is the truth.

The artist's medium is not reality, but dreams. I don't mean "dreams" in the sense of made-up bullshit. I mean dreams as the X-ray of truth—truth seen through and seen for what it really is, truth boiled down to its essence.

The conventional truism is "Write what you know." But something mysterious and wonderful happens when we write what we *don't* know. The Muse enters the arena. Stuff comes out of us from a source we can neither name nor locate.

Where is it coming from? The "unconscious"? The "field of potentiality"?

I don't know.

But I've had the same experience over and over. When I write something that really happened, people read it and say, "Sounds phony."

When I pull something completely out of thin air, I hear, "Wow, that was so real!"

THE ARTIST'S JOURNEY
PROGRESSES BY INCREMENTS

Album #1 (1964)

Route 66

I'm a King Bee

Can I Get a Witness?

I Just Wanna Make Love to You

Album #2 (1964)

Under the Boardwalk

Susie Q

Confessing the Blues

It's All Over Now

Album #5 (1965)

Satisfaction

The Last Time

Play with Fire

The Under-Assistant West Coast Promotion Man

Album #11 (1968)

Sympathy for the Devil

No Expectations

Street Fighting Man

Salt of the Earth

Album #12 (1969)
Gimme Shelter
Love in Vain
Midnight Rambler
You Can't Always Get What You Want

The subject stays the same, but the artists have peeled back the onion from the surface to delve to a place deep, deep within the core.

Chekhov did it this way, as did Fitzgerald and Hemingway, Tolstoy and Turgenev, all the way back to Aeschylus, Sophocles, and Euripides.

The artist mines the same vein over and over. He just digs deeper over time.

THE ARTIST'S JOURNEY IS
ABOUT ACCESSING THE UNCONSCIOUS

You can attend the Iowa Writers' Workshop, get a degree in Literature from Harvard, hang on your wall a framed MFA from the USC School of Cinematic Arts. You can serve with the Navy SEALs in Afghanistan, survive heroin addiction in East St. Louis. You can break your back at hard labor, break your heart in love, break your balls in the school of hard knocks.

None of it will do a damn bit of good if you can't sit down and open the pipeline to your Muse.

The artist's journey is about that.

Nothing else matters.

Nothing else counts.

THE ARTIST'S JOURNEY LASTS THE REST OF YOUR LIFE

There is no other journey in this lifetime after the artist's journey (other than, perhaps, the transition to the next life).

Once you board this train, you're on it to the end of the line.

BOOK TWO

LEVELING UP

A Body of Work

A BODY OF WORK

This is my nineteenth book.

Looking back, here's the Big Takeaway:

> I never had any idea, before I wrote a book,
> that I was going to write it. Or, perhaps more
> accurately, that I was going to write *that spe-
> cific book*. The book always came out of no-
> where and always took me by surprise.

Let me express this a different way.

> No matter what a writer or artist may tell you, they
> have no clue what they're doing before they do it—
> and, for the most part, *while* they're doing it.

Or another way:

> Everything we produce as artists comes from
> a source beyond our conscious awareness.

Jackson Browne once said that he writes to find out what he thinks. (Wait, it was Joan Didion who said that ... no, Stephen King said it too.)

I do the same, and you do too, whether you realize it or not.

The key pronoun here is *you*.

Who is this "you"?

The second and third theses of this book are:

1. "You," meaning the writer of your books, is not you. Not the "you" you think of as yourself.

2. This "second you" is smarter than you are. A lot smarter. This second "you" is the real you.

WHERE DO BOOKS/SONGS/MOVIES COME FROM?

My long-held belief is that an artist's identity is revealed by the work she or he produces.

Writers write to *discover* themselves. (Again, whether they realize it or not.)

But who is this self they seek to discover?

It is none other than that "second you"—that wiser "you," that true, pure, waterproof, self-propelled, self-contained "you."

Every work we produce as artists comes from this second "you."

Our first "you" is nothing but the vehicle that contains (and initially conceals) our real you.

WHO R U?

I've read a dozen different versions of Stanislavski's famous Three Questions, i.e., the queries an actor must ask him- or herself before playing any scene. Here's my version:

> Who am I?
> Why am I here?
> What do I want?

The second two are pretty easy. It's the first that's the killer.

> Who am I?

An actor can answer that question like this: "I'm Ophelia. I'm Hamlet's sweetheart and potential bride, etc."

What about you and me?

We have to answer that question not on the stage and in a pre-written role, but in our own lives and in our own art.

> "Tell me who you are, Junah. Who, in your deepest parts, when all that is unauthentic has been stripped away. Are you your name, Rannulph Junah? Will that hit this shot for you?

Are you your illustrious forebears? Will they hit it?

"Are you your roles, Junah? Scion, soldier, Southerner? Husband, father, lover? Slayer of the foe in battle, comforter of the friend at home? Are you your virtues, Junah, or your sins? Your deeds, your feats? Are you your dreams or your nightmares? Tell me, Junah. Can you hit the ball with any of these?"

We said earlier that a writer or an artist has no idea what she's doing when she is initially seized by an idea.

I certainly had no clue when this passage of dialogue appeared on the page in *The Legend of Bagger Vance*. I didn't plan it. It wasn't in any outline.

How did it get there?

What happened?

What happened was the "me" that wasn't me, knowing that this issue was central to my evolution as a writer and as a human being, broke through like a dream and pushed those sentences onto the page.

THE WORLD THE ARTIST LIVES IN

Here's my model of the universe in a nutshell (we'll get into this more deeply in Part Three):

> The universe exists on at least two levels. The first is the material world, the visible physical sphere in which you and I dwell.

Then there's the second level.
The higher level.

> The second level exists "above" the first but permeates the latter at all times and in all instances. This second level is the invisible world, the plane of the as-yet-unmanifested, the sphere of pure potentiality.

Upon this level dwells that which will be, but is not yet.
Call this level the Unconscious, the Soul, the Self, the Superconscious.

THE ARTIST'S SKILL

What exactly does an artist do? The writer, the dancer, the filmmaker ... what, precisely, does their work consist of?

> They shuttle from Level #1 to Level #2 and back again.

That's it.

That's their skill.

Twyla Tharp in her dance studio, Quentin Tarantino at his keyboard, Bob Dylan when he picks up a guitar or sits down at a piano. They perform this simple but miraculous act a thousand, ten thousand times a day.

> They enter the Second World and come back to the First with something that had never existed in the First World before.

A machine can't do that.

A supercomputer packed with the most powerful AI system can't do that.

In all of Creation, only two creatures can do that.

Gods.

And you and I.

THE CONTOUR OF THE ARTIST'S LIFE

From the epiphanal moment at the end of her hero's journey, the artist's life is about the works she will produce. These taken in sum will comprise her body of work. They're her "oeuvre."

They're also her destiny.

If she does it right, they will constitute upon completion a pretty fair expression of why she was put on Earth. They'll define who she is. They will be her "gift for the people."

But here's the interesting part.

Each work (or, more exactly, the artist's inner odyssey as she labors to produce each work) will be a hero's journey in its own right.

EACH INCREMENT OF THE ARTIST'S JOURNEY IS A HERO'S JOURNEY

We experience our life as dull and ordinary. But beneath the surface, something powerful and transformative is brewing.

Suddenly the light bulb goes off. We've got a new idea! An idea for a novel, a movie, a startup ...

Except immediately we perceive the downside. We become daunted. Our idea is too risky, we fear. We're afraid we can't pull it off. We hesitate, until ...

We're having drinks with a friend. We tell her our idea. "I love it," she says. "You've gotta do it."

Fortified, we rally.

We commit.

We begin.

This is the pattern for the genesis of any creative work. It's also, in Joseph Campbell terms, "the Ordinary World," "The Call," "Refusal of the Call," "Meeting with the Mentor," and "Crossing the Threshold."

In other words, the first five stages of the hero's journey.

Keep going. As you progress on your project, you'll hit every other Campbellian beat, right down to the finish and release/publication, i.e., "The Return," bearing a "Gift for the People."

This pattern will hold true for the rest of your life, through every novel, movie, dance, drama, work of architecture, etc. you produce.

Every work is its own hero's journey.

EACH TRIP FROM LEVEL #1 TO LEVEL #2 IS A HERO'S JOURNEY

We said a few chapters ago that the artist's skill is to shuttle from the material sphere to the sphere of potentiality and back again.

Each one of those trips is a hero's journey.

Jay-Z in his studio may complete ten thousand hero's journeys a day.

You do too.

Ordinary World to The Call to Refusal of Call to Threshold to Extraordinary World and back again.

Watch yourself today as you bang out your five hundred words. You'll see the hero's journey over and over.

ANOTHER WAY OF
LOOKING AT RESISTANCE

If each of our ten thousand daily excursions from Level #1 to Level #2 is in fact a mini-hero's journey, then what is Resistance?

Resistance is a mini-Refusal of the Call.

Odysseus, hailed by Agamemnon to the great adventure of the Trojan War, pretends to be insane so he can evade this summons. Rocky's immediate response to the once-in-a-lifetime chance to fight the champ is to turn down the offer. Even Luke Skywalker, the son of a Jedi knight, balks at Princess Leia's cry for help, delivered in hologram form by R2-D2.

The Call is scary.

No wonder our initial impulse is to hide from it.

How do we overcome this moment of weakness and hesitation?

You and I, each morning (and ten thousand more times that day), must create our own "meeting with the mentor." There, acting as our own Obi-Wan Kenobi, we kick our reluctant butts across the Threshold and shuttle off to Level #2.

THE HERO'S JOURNEY IS REHEARSAL FOR THE ARTIST'S JOURNEY

Our real-life hero's journey—the passage we've undergone in the material universe that has carried us to our "return home"—is practice for this, the next stage in our maturation, the artist's journey.

Write your first novel. Produce your first movie. Yeah, it's true that you've never done it before. But you've had practice. You've already endured all the trials and passed through all the stages.

You did it on your hero's journey.

You crossed the threshold, you encountered allies and enemies, you entered the inmost cave, you've died and been reborn. And you've made your return safely to the place from which you set forth.

The stages of the artist's journey are the same stages you've rehearsed (even though you had no idea you were doing that) on your hero's journey.

What, then, are the stages of the artist's journey?

What is their nature?

How are they different from the stages of the hero's journey?

THE MYSTICAL AND
THE MATTER OF FACT

The artist's journey is enacted on two opposite but linked planes: the mystical and the matter of fact.

(Or, if you prefer, left brain/right brain, Dionysian/Apollonian.)

The artist's journey is an alchemical admixture of the airy-fairy and the workshop-practical. On the one hand we're teaching ourselves to surrender to the moment, to inspiration, to intuition, to imagination. On the other, a huge part of our day is about discovering and mastering the nuts-and-bolts mechanics of how to reproduce in the real world the stuff we have encountered in the sphere of the imagination.

Monet spent years figuring out how to affix blobs of paint to canvas in such a way as to produce the illusion of sunlight reflecting off the surface of water. This was blue-collar labor. Trial and error. Seen from the outside, it was the most tedious, excruciating activity imaginable.

Yet at the same time the process was absolutely mystical. What went on in Monet's mind as he wrestled month after month, year after year with a problem that had bewitched and confounded painters for centuries?

Monet, like every artist, was working simultaneously on both planes.

On the Dionysian he could see in his mind's eye exactly how sunlight bounced off the curvilinear perimeter of a lily pad. On the Apollonian he was thinking, "If I apply a double-thick blob of gentian violet with a medium pallet knife and twist it left-handed so that the weightiest section of the blob accretes on the right side, then studio daylight reflecting off that, in juxtaposition to the 40/60 mixture of puce and fuchsia of the adjacent blob, should create the exact illusion I'm seeking."

Like an alchemist laboring to turn lead into gold, the artist operates simultaneously on the planes of the ethereal and the elemental.

THE MATTER OF FACT PLANE
OF THE ARTIST'S JOURNEY

In the sphere we call the artist's journey, we "get down to business." Crazy-time is over. We have wasted enough years avoiding our calling.

Our aim now is to discover our gift, our voice, our subject. We know now that we have one—and we are driven passionately to identify it and to bring it forth in the real world with optimum wallop.

Here's Rosanne Cash from *Composed:*

> From that moment I changed the way I approached songwriting, I changed how I sang, I changed my work ethic, and I changed my life. The strong desire to become a better songwriter dovetailed perfectly with my budding friendship with John Stewart, who had written "Runaway Train" for [my album] *King's Record Shop.* John encouraged me to expand the subject matter in my songs, as well as my choice of language and my mind. I played new songs for him and if he thought it

was too "perfect," which was anathema to him, he would say, over and over, "but where is the MADNESS, Rose?" I started looking for the madness. I sought out Marge Rivingston in New York to work on my voice and I started training, as if I were a runner, in both technique and stamina. Oddly, it turned out that Marge also worked with Linda [Ronstadt], which I didn't know when I sought her out. I started paying attention to everything, both in the studio and out. If I found myself drifting off into daydreams—an old, entrenched habit—I pulled myself awake and back into the present moment. Instead of toying with ideas, I examined them, and I tested the authenticity of my instincts musically. I stretched my attention span consciously. I read books on writing by Natalie Goldberg and Carolyn Heilbrun and began to self-edit and refine more, and went deeper into every process involved with writing and musicianship. I realized I had earlier been working only within my known range—never pushing far outside the comfort zone to take any real risks ... I started painting, so I could learn about the absence of words and sound, and why I needed them. I took painting lessons from Sharon Orr, who had a series of classes at a studio called Art and Soul.

I remained completely humbled by the dream [that had been the epiphanal moment at the end of my hero's journey], and it stayed with me through every waking hour of completing *King's Record Shop* ... I vowed the next record would reflect my new commitment. Rodney [Crowell, my then-husband] was at the top of his game as a record producer, but I had come to feel curiously like a neophyte in the studio after the dream. Everything seemed new, frightening, and tremendously exciting.

On the matter-of-fact plane we set ourselves the task, not just of learning our craft, but also of mastering those professional capacities that are even more basic. In the succeeding chapters we'll attempt an index of these fundamental skills.

A FURTHER NOTE RE RESISTANCE

The stages of the artist's journey share one fundamental quality.

They are all battles against Resistance.

Resistance meaning fear.

Resistance meaning distraction.

Resistance meaning temptation.

Resistance meaning the aggressive self-perpetuation of the ego.

Resistance meaning the terror the psyche experiences at the prospect of encountering the Self, i.e., the soul, the unconscious, the superconscious.

On the artist's journey we develop skills. Skills we did not have before.

We teach ourselves these skills.

We apprentice ourselves to others wiser than we are.

We are fortifying ourselves, training ourselves against fear, boredom, laziness, arrogance, self-inflation, complacency.

Our aim is to make ourselves masters, not just of our craft, but also of ourselves.

When we underwent our original hero's journey we were neophytes. We had no idea what we were doing.

Now we are different.

We return to the fire determined to do it better this time.

AN INDEX OF BASIC SKILLS

What follows is my own idiosyncratic inventory of the essential (and mandatory) skills that the artist acquires on his or her artist's journey.

THE ARTIST LEARNS
HOW TO START

This sounds so obvious, so self-evident. And yet ...

Not one aspirant in a hundred, in my experience, is capable of pulling the trigger, jumping out of the airplane, diving head-first into the icy pool.

THE ARTIST LEARNS
HOW TO KEEP GOING

The phrase "Act Two problems" has become a cliché. Why? Because the winnowing scythe of Resistance cuts down so many aspiring artists right here, in mid-odyssey. Here's David Mamet from *Three Uses of the Knife*.

> In his analysis of world myth, Joseph Campbell calls this period *in the belly of the beast*— the time which is not the beginning and not the end, the time in which the artist and the protagonist doubt themselves and wish the journey had never begun.
>
> ... How many times have we heard (and said): Yes, I know that I was cautioned, that the way would become difficult and I would want to quit, that such was inevitable, and that *at exactly this point* the battle would be lost or won. Yes, I know all that, but those who cautioned me *could not* have foreseen the magnitude of the specific difficulties *I* am experiencing at this point—difficulties which must, sadly, but I have no choice, force me to resign the struggle (and have a drink, a cigarette, an affair, a rest), in short, to declare failure.

THE ARTIST LEARNS
HOW TO FINISH

Notice please that these first three skills exist *in relation to Resistance*. They are about overcoming Resistance.

Before our hero's journey, we had never even started a project. (We had fabricated some excuse to put it off.) Or if we had started, we bailed in the middle or choked at the end.

But now we are different. We have been toughened by our real-life hero's journey. We will not yield this time. We will find our way over, under, around, or through the obstacles, no matter what.

Note too that these first three skills are aspects of professionalism. These same skills are mastered by the professional athlete, the professional businessperson, or anyone (including moms and dads and their own kids in school) who is committed to an aspiration or a calling.

These skills and others we'll delineate in subsequent chapters constitute the infrastructure of the artist's power. They are the tracks along which his locomotive rolls and the foundation upon which the edifices of his city rise.

THE ARTIST LEARNS
HOW TO HANG ON

I worked on a movie that took seventeen years to get made. When the Writers Guild opened the arbitration process for screen credit, more than thirty screenwriters filed.

One writer, the co-originator of the project, had been on the picture from the start. Even when he was fired and other writers or other teams of writers were brought in, he stayed attached as a producer. (He made half a dozen other movies in the interim, by the way.)

He was brought back four different times as a writer. He was there at the finish. He got the credit. He saw the movie made.

Was he crazy?

Maybe.

But he knew how to hang on.

THE ARTIST LEARNS
HOW TO LET GO

I was visiting my friend Robert Bidner at his studio in Brooklyn. As Bob was showing me the paintings he was currently working on—about half a dozen on easels in varying stages of completion—I noticed another sheaf of canvases stacked against a wall in back.

"Those are my clinkers," Bob said.

In the days when homes were heated by coal, he explained, every load inevitably contained one or two lumps that refused to burn.

Those were called clinkers.

I couldn't stop my eye from returning to those abandoned paintings. I asked Bob if he ever hauled any back out and tried again to make them work.

"I used to," he said.

Then he shook his head.

"You gotta know when to let go."

THE ARTIST LEARNS
HOW TO BE ALONE

She trains herself to find emotional and spiritual sustenance *in the work*.

Her need for third-party validation attenuates. She may still ask you of her work, "What do you think?" But she evaluates your response within the framework of her own self-grounded assessment of her gifts and aspirations—and of how well or poorly she herself believes she has used the one in the service of the other.

THE ARTIST LEARNS
HOW TO WORK WITH OTHERS

She lets go of the need to plaster her name over everything.

It's fun to jam, she decides. And even more fun when the finished product is better than any of the constituents could have produced on their own. She sees the beauty now in "Rodgers & Hammerstein" and "Jagger & Richards."

Note please, as we delineate these skills, that their absence is the sign of the amateur.

An amateur can't start, can't keep going, can't finish, can't work alone, can't work with others.

We ourselves were amateurs before our hero's journey. That ordeal has chastened us. We have peered into the abyss and it has slapped us back into reality. We might not, now, *want* to start, want to keep going, want to finish, want to work alone, want to collaborate—but we have confronted the alternative and it has scared us straight.

THE ARTIST LEARNS
EMOTIONAL DISTANCE

I used to write novels that read like personal journals. To slog through them was excruciating, even for me.

The artist learns to detach himself from his material expectations. He learns to separate his personal identity from the response to his work.

J. D. Salinger understands that he is not Holden Caulfield.

George Lucas is not Luke Skywalker.

The artist is not the book. Or the movie. Or the startup.

The artist learns that she is not to be held accountable to her first "you," but to her second.

This second self, her *real* self, is the true audience and the true judge of her work.

The artist learns to serve this second self, not the box office tallies in the *Hollywood Reporter* or the bestseller list in *The New York Times*.

THE ARTIST LEARNS
HOW TO HANDLE REJECTION

Can you see the theme running through these chapters?

The theme is maturity.

The theme is professionalism.

The theme is mental toughness.

Every one of these skills (and the ones in chapters to follow) requires of the artist a profound shift in perspective and a quantum breakthrough in emotional self-possession. This work is hard. It hurts. We are beating our heads into a wall, hoping to teach ourselves to stop.

You may scoff at what I'm about to say, but we are becoming Zen masters.

We're training ourselves to be Jedi knights.

I know, I know. "Every writer and artist I know," you say, "is a lush, a sex addict, an emotional infant, simultaneously a tyrant and a coward, an egomaniac, a depressive and a flaming, incurable asshole."

That may indeed be true.

But that's not us.

That's not you and me.

We are not going to be beaten by a pile of rejection slips (or even that excruciating close call that put us within inches of our material and artistic dream but then was snatched away at the fatal instant for reasons that were inane, arbitrary, or nonexistent altogether).

No one said the artist's journey was easy or without pain.

THE ARTIST LEARNS
HOW TO HANDLE PRAISE

Before, she would have been seduced by that rave in *The New Yorker*. It would've gone to her head. She would have become insufferable.

The ordeal of her real-life hero's journey, however, has taught her humility. "Yeah, yeah," she thinks as she assesses the critic's over-the-moon adulation. "And what'll you write next time?"

She accepts the plaudits with gratitude and, then goes back to work.

THE ARTIST LEARNS
HOW TO HANDLE PANIC

I interviewed a test pilot once. He told me that over the course of his career he had put more than two hundred and fifty airplanes into deliberate tailspins to test the crafts' physical limits.

"Of course you are scared," he said. "But you understand what causes a tailspin. And you know how to pull out of it."

The artist learns that panic strikes at that point in a project when a creative breakthrough is imminent. Panic is Resistance pulling out the stops to keep us from ascending to the next level.

The artist, like the test pilot, learns to stay cool and keep flying the plane.

THE ARTIST LEARNS TO GIVE UP

In Eugen Herrigel's 1953 classic, *Zen in the Art of Archery*, the author, a deeply serious student of Zen Buddhism, travels to Japan and enrolls in an academy of archery.

In this school the physical act of drawing the bow and loosing the arrow (as also in other schools with meditation, martial arts, the study of calligraphy or flower arrangement or mastery of the tea ceremony) is not undertaken for its own sake but as a portal to insight, to enlightenment.

For Herrigel, the process came down to one challenge: the simple act of releasing the bowstring.

Herrigel could not get it right.

He would draw the bow with the fingers of his right hand (in Japan this act is performed with the thumb and forefinger) pulling the string back to its full stretch. Then he would release the string, shooting the arrow toward the target.

Hundreds, thousands of times Herrigel attempted to do this, but always his instructor found fault with his technique.

"The bowstring," declared Herrigel's teacher, "must release itself without your will or consciousness. You are thinking too much. You are trying too hard."

Herrigel was instructed to hold the stretch until the string escaped from his fingers *by itself*, so that the release came to him as a surprise.

The setting for the student of an unsolvable riddle, a *koan*, is at the heart of the teaching of Zen.

The idea is to exhaust the aspirant's will, to extinguish his ego, to break down his stubborn, prideful mind and his compulsion to control the event. The moment of breakdown is the moment of breakthrough.

But how do you do it?

How do you try and not-try?

How do you do and not-do?

How do you find your subject?

How do you find your voice?

How do you find your point of view?

THE ARTIST LEARNS TO GO
BEYOND WHAT SHE KNOWS

The artist can feel it when she's working beyond her limits. Her blood thrills. She loves it.

This is the rush of working in the arts. It's why she came to this dance.

We can sense it, you and I, when we're playing it safe. And we know, too, when we've stepped out beyond the light of the campfire.

Out there is where all good things happen.

THE ARTIST LEARNS TO BE BRAVE

Elite warriors are trained to "run toward the sound of the guns."

The artist lives by that principle too.

What project terrifies her most? What work is she certain she can never pull off? What role will push her past her limits, take her into places she has never gone? What journey will carry her off the map entirely?

The artist hears the guns. She feels the battle lines inside her and she senses which quarter of the field terrifies her most.

She goes there.

She runs there.

THE ARTIST LEARNS TO
KEEP THE PRESSURE ON

Every work resists you. It wrestles against you like an alligator. It kicks and bucks you like a bronco.

The artist learns to "sit chilly," as the renowned equestrienne Sue Sally Hale used to say.

He answers the bell every round. He refuses to go down. He will keep the pressure on week after week, month after month, year after year.

He knows the oak will fall.

The enemy will tire.

The gator will roll over and quit.

THE ARTIST LEARNS TO KILL

The struggle between the artist and her work is a duel to the death.

One of them is going to surrender.

One of them will go belly up.

INDEX OF SKILLS, CONTINUED

The artist learns how to help others and how to be helped. She learns how to steal and how to give away.

She studies the marketplace and comes to understand it (as much as it can be understood).

She acquires perspective on herself and her work and the place of her work within the field of her contemporaries and of those who have gone before.

She studies the work of the masters who have preceded her. She learns to appreciate them and to respect the gifts they have bequeathed to her.

She acquires humility and she gains self-belief.

She learns to self-motivate.

To self-validate.

To self-reinforce.

And to self-evaluate.

She has become a professional.

Now when someone asks her what she does, she answers without hesitation, "I'm an artist."

THE ARTIST LEARNS TO
COMMIT FOR A LIFETIME

It's easy for Bob Dylan or Neil Young to say, "I'm never going back to work in the bean fields."

What about you and me?

Can we say it and mean it?

"BUT WHERE'S
THE MADNESS, ROSE?"

Now we come to the mystical level. The right brain. The Dionysian.

What are the stages of the artist's journey on this plane?

THE BLANK PAGE

We hear (and we know, ourselves) of the terror that writers experience when confronting the blank page.

Rather than face this, they will delay, dilate, demur, procrastinate, rationalize, cop out, self-justify, self-exonerate, not to mention become drunks and drug addicts, cheat on their spouses, lose themselves on Facebook, Instagram and Twitter, and in general destroy not only their bodies and minds but their souls as well.

Why?

What's so scary about an 8 1/2 X 11 sheet of uncoated bond?

ENCOUNTER WITH THE UNCONSCIOUS

What's scary is that, in order to write (or paint or compose or shoot film), we have two choices:

1. We can work from our ego-minds, in which case we will burst blood vessels and suffer cerebral hernias, only to produce tedious, mediocre, derivative crap.
2. We can shift our platform of effort from our conscious mind to our unconscious.

Which one do you think we're most terrified of?

THE MISNOMER OF THE UNCONSCIOUS

The Unconscious (to use the term as Freud originally defined it) is unconscious only *to us*.

We are unconscious of its contents.

But the Unconscious mind is *not* unconscious to itself or of itself.

The Unconscious is wide awake.

It knows exactly what it is and exactly what it's doing.

(And it's pretty pissed off at being called "the Unconscious.")

THE SUPERCONSCIOUS

Instead let's call it the Superconscious. That's what it is.

The superconscious is that part of our psyche that knows where we put our keys when our conscious mind is certain we've lost them.

It's that part of our brain that divines, in .0001 second, that that very attractive, bewitching, charismatic new person we just met is big-time trouble.

It's that part of our mind that wakes us at precisely the minute we set our mental alarm clocks to.

It's that part of our consciousness, if we're a wildebeest, that guides us infallibly from the Serengeti to the Maasai Mara, or, if we're a Monarch butterfly (with a brain the size of the head of a pin), three thousand miles from eastern North America to the Sierra Madre mountains in Mexico, even though not a single butterfly in the migration has made the trip before.

The superconscious is that part of our psyche that dreams, that intuits. According to Jung, it's that part that lies adjacent to and is linked with the "Divine Ground."

The superconscious is the part of our mind that speaks in our true voice, knows our true subject, and makes decisions from our true point of view.

The superconscious is the part of our psyche that enabled Einstein to conceive the Special Theory of Relativity and

Steph Curry to hit nineteen three-pointers in a row with an opponent's hand in his face on every shot.

Tolstoy didn't write *War and Peace*. His superconscious did.

Picasso didn't paint *Guernica*. His superconscious did.

Trey Parker and Matt Stone didn't create *South Park*, their superconsciouses did.

I've got a superconscious, and so do you.

Our problem, you and I, is that we don't know how to access it or, if we do, we're too terrified to take the chance.

The artist's journey, as we've said, is about linking the conscious mind to the superconscious. It's about learning to shuttle back and forth between the two.

WHAT IS THE ARTIST AFRAID OF?

The artist is afraid of the unknown.

She's afraid of letting go. Afraid of finding out what's "in there." Or "out there."

I'm not speaking here of unearthing within ourselves hitherto-unknown sordid, depraved, vile, degenerate urges. I don't mean the fear of realizing that we're all child molesters at heart or that we would have joined the Nazi Party if we'd lived in Germany in 1934.

The artist is afraid of finding out who she is.

This fear, I suspect, is more about finding we are *greater* than we think than discovering that we're lesser.

What if, God help us, we actually have talent?

What if we truly do possess a gift?

What will we do then?

THINKING WITH OUR SECOND MIND

What exactly are we trying to accomplish on our artist's journey?

We're trying to *think as our "second selves,"* not as our first (and not as anyone else's self either), and thus to speak in our true voice.

We are teaching ourselves to step off the platform of our front-mind, our ego-consciousness (and self-consciousness) and board the train to the next level, the unconscious, the superconscious, the Self, the Muse.

As in zazen meditation, the student is seeking to sit without thinking. To empty her mind of all ego-spawned "thought"(which is really the mindless chatter of Resistance) until her consciousness becomes as clear as a glass of formerly muddy water after the silty particles have settled to the bottom.

This is exactly what the artist does when she sets her brush to the canvas.

It's what the musician does when he places his fingers on the keys.

The artist and the writer enter the Void with nothing and come back with something.

THE VOID

How does a writer write a scene, or a choreographer design a dance sequence?

They start with nothing. An intention only.

They reach into the void and pull out a sentence, a first step.

They go back in, like the actor James Spader reaching through the liquid-metallic membrane in the movie *Stargate*. They pull their arm back out with the next sentence or the next dance move.

Now they have momentum. They feel a glimmer of courage.

They reach through the membrane again, this time up to the elbow.

Next: the shoulder.

They step all the way through.

Their hearts are hammering.

It's terrifying releasing one's hold on the known.

THE OTHER SIDE

What's on the far side of the Stargate?

We are.

The writer and the dancer and the filmmaker ourselves.

Our selves wait there, breathless and trembling, pulling on the ego-writer and ego-dancer and ego-filmmaker with all their strength.

"Come through! Hold out your hand! You're safe!"

THE AMAZON MIND

In *Last of the Amazons*, I tried to imagine the ancient race of female warriors.

Here's a description of the Amazon mode of thinking, offered by one of the characters in the book, a young Athenian who has traveled to the Amazon homeland near the Black Sea and lived for a time among this legendary all-female culture.

> The Amazons have no word for "I." The notion of the autonomous individual has no place in their conception of the universe. Their thinking, if one could call it that, is entirely instinctual and collective. They think like a herd of horses or a flock of swallows, which seem to apprehend and respond with one mind, acting intuitively and instantaneously in the moment.
>
> When an Amazon speaks, she will pause frequently, often for long moments. She is seeking the right word. But she does not *consciously* search for this, as you or I might, rummaging within the catalog of our mind. Rather she is waiting, as a hunter might at the burrow of her quarry, until the correct word

arises of itself as from some primal spring of consciousness. The process, it seems, is more akin to dreaming than to waking awareness.

To our Greek eyes, this habit of pausing and waiting makes the speaker appear dull-witted, even dense, and many among our compatriots have lost patience in the event or, concluding that these horsewomen of the plains are a race of savages, have given up entirely on attempting to communicate with them.

To the Amazons, of course, it is we Hellenes who are the witless ones, whose "civilized" consciousness has lost access to the well of wisdom and sense upon which the plainswoman readily draws, and who as a result are cut off from the immediate apprehension of the moment, immured within our own narrow, fearful, greedy, self-infatuated minds.

The Amazon mind as imagined in this passage is not far from the artist's mind when she is at work.

THE ARTIST BELIEVES
IN A DIFFERENT REALITY

Did you ever see the Meg Ryan-Nicholas Cage movie, *City of Angels*?

In *City of Angels* (screenplay by Dana Stevens based on the film *Wings of Desire*, screenplay by Wim Wenders and Peter Handke), human characters go about their lives oblivious of the cohort of angels—all handsome, male and female, dressed in stylish, duster-length coats—who attend upon them and are present about them at all times, often standing invisibly directly at their shoulders.

That's my world.

That's what I see.

Everything I do is based upon that reality.

THE ARTIST GROUNDS HERSELF
IN A DIFFERENT REALITY

When an individual "gets saved" (or when an alcoholic or addict makes the decision to get sober), the ground of her being shifts.

Her psychic core relocates.

Her identity no longer centers itself in her ego. It packs up and moves to a different quadrant of her psyche.

For the artist, that level is the unconscious, the Jungian Self, the Muse, the superconscious. Henry Miller again:

> I didn't dare to think of anything then except the "facts." To get beneath the facts I would have had to be an artist, and one doesn't become an artist overnight. First you have to be crushed, to have your conflicting points of view annihilated. You have to be wiped out as a human being in order to be born again an individual. You have to be carbonized and mineralized in order to work upwards from the last common denominator of the self. You have to get beyond pity in order to feel from the very roots of your being.

THE ARTIST SHUTTLES BACK AND FORTH BETWEEN REALITIES

Have you ever observed your mind as you write or paint or compose?

I've watched mine. Here's what I see:

I see my awareness (another phrase might be "platform of effort") shuttle back and forth, like the subway between Times Square and Grand Central Terminal, from my conscious mind to my unconscious, my superconscious.

The *Stargate* image is very close to what it feels like. Sometimes I stick just my hand through, sometimes my whole arm. Most of the time my whole body goes through.

The process is to me one of those everyday miracles, simultaneously mind-bending in its implications and common as dirt. Like the act of giving birth, it is at the same time miraculous and everyday.

Another image I like is of a child sitting beside a shallow stream. You, the artist, are the child. The words you will write, the pictures you will paint, the photos you will take ... those are the bright, pretty pebbles sitting right there before you at the bottom of the stream. You reach down, through the surface of the water (you can't see *exactly* what the pebbles look like because of the refraction of the light), and you pull up a handful.

The stream bottom is one reality.

Sunlight and air is the other.

One is mysterious, the other matter of fact.

One requires faith, the other reason.

We plunge our hand through the surface, not sure what we'll find.

We pull our hand back and examine what we've got. Good? Bad? Worth keeping? To be put where? Utilized how?

In a four-hour working day, the writer shuttles between realities a thousand times, two thousand, ten thousand. So does the choreographer, the editor, the software writer.

This shuttling is her primary skill.

It's her bread and butter.

It's what she does.

DO WE HAVE A
PERSONAL IDENTITY?

Buddhists don't think so.

The concept of the individual personality (and thus a voice that you or I could call "ours") is in Buddhist thought an illusion.

True mind, the Buddha taught, is empty. Clear as glass. Pellucid as the air through which sunlight passes.

A Samurai warrior, guided by this Buddhist precept, does not prepare for battle by rehearsing mentally, by planning, or by filling his mind with schemes and intentions.

Instead he empties his mind.

His belief is that this "no-mind" knows more than his conscious ego-mind and will respond perfectly every time in the moment.

This is the voice you and I are seeking as artists.

The voice of no-voice.

The voice of our second self.

THE SURPRISE OF
FINDING OUR VOICE

I have a recurring dream.

A good dream.

In the dream I'm in my house (or some place that I recognize as my house even though technically it doesn't look exactly like my actual house) when I realize that I'm occupying a room that I have never been in before. An additional room. An expanded room.

Sometimes this room takes up an entire floor. I'll be standing there, looking at crystal chandeliers and rows of pool tables extending for half a block, with music playing and people partying, and I'll think "Wow, I had no idea this part of the house even existed. How could I have missed it all this time?"

That house is my psyche. The new rooms are parts of me I have never, till I dreamt them, been aware of.

We find our voice that same way. Project by project. Subject by subject. Observing in happy amazement as a new "us" pops out each time.

THE SURPRISE OF FINDING OUR SUBJECT

I wonder if Stephen King knew when he was a kid that horror, the supernatural, and speculative fiction would be his métier.

I can testify for myself that I had no clue whatsoever that I would be writing about the things I wound up writing about.

It's as though some Cosmic Assignment Desk, with access to our test scores and aptitude charts (that we ourselves have never seen) is suddenly calling us forward and with absolute authority handing us our orders packet.

The artist's journey is nothing if not full of surprises.

WHAT THESE SURPRISES MEAN

The artist on her journey opens the pipeline to the unconscious, the Muse, the superconscious.

With this, every prior assumption flies out the window—who our parents told us we were, what our teachers imagined we'd become, even what we ourselves believe we are or will turn out to be.

The Muse tells us who we *really* are and what our subject *really* is.

No wonder these feel like surprises. They are voices that we never knew we had, rooms and wings in our house that we never knew existed.

When we say the artist's journey is a process of self-discovery, this is what we mean.

BOOK THREE

BEYOND THE HORIZON

The Higher Realm

HOW THE WORLD WORKS

Let's return to the model of the universe we touched upon in the chapter titled The World the Artist Lives In.

This is my own personal, idiosyncratic, totally unprovable Theory of Everything.

1.   The universe exists on at least two levels.

The universe may in fact exist on an infinite number of levels. But for sure it exists on at least two.

2.   Level One = The Material World

This is the Physical Universe that you and I inhabit every day. In this world, we have bodies. We exist in physical form. Time is real. Space is real. Death is real.

3.   Level Two = The Higher Realm

This level exists "above" us. It is invisible, immaterial, incorporeal. We cannot touch this level or see it or measure it. We cannot visit it. We cannot command it or summon it.

But we can feel it. We can sense it. We "remember" it, though most of us cannot recall from where.

If we were living in ancient Greece, we would call this level "Olympus." On this plane, time does not exist. Nor space. Nor death. The gods are immortal. They travel "swift as thought."

If we were in Sunday School, we'd call this level "heaven." The saints live here. The angels. God is here. It's the level we pray to.

If we were Native Americans, we'd think of this level as the dwelling place of the ancestors, the home of our spirit guides and animal mentors. When we go on a vision quest, this is the level we're seeking to reach.

If we're yogis in India, or mystics in any culture, we would seek this level through meditation, through ascetic practices, through renunciation of the senses, and through the ingestion of psychotropic plants, teas, herbs, etc.

This Higher Realm is the level upon which "the future" is formed. It is the plane of What Will Be, the dimension of potentiality.

This level is the plane you and I are seeking to access when we write, paint, dance, start a business, etc.

THE HIGHER REALM FOR ARTISTS

If we're artists, we think of this higher level as Mount Parnon, the dwelling place of the Muses. This level is the source of inspiration. From this level come all creativity and all art.

If we're artists, our first order of business is to learn how to open the channel between this level and ourselves.

THE NESHAMA

In the Kabbalah, there's a name for this higher level. It's called the *neshama*. The soul.

The neshama, kabbalists believe, is neither neutral nor inert. It is active.

In Jewish mysticism it is believed that the neshama is constantly trying to communicate with us. The higher realm is reaching down, with positive intention, seeking to touch us and inform us on the material plane.

At the same time we on the material plane are reaching up to the neshama. You might call this action "prayer," although it manifests itself in many other ways.

The choreographer, for instance, may reach out to the neshama, asking, "What's my next dance? How do I solve this third movement?" The painter calls upon the neshama in her own way, as do the filmmaker and the restaurateur and the software designer.

The office worker stuck in her cubicle may find herself reaching out to her neshama (without calling it by this name of course) asking, "Should I quit? Should I stay? What should I do?"

When we quiet ourselves and try to listen for that "still, small voice" inside us, what we're trying to reach is the neshama, the Muse. Our soul. Our Self.

The soul, we feel certain, has the answers. It knows best.

But there's a catch.

RESISTANCE

Though you and I as embodied souls exist here on the material plane, our nature compels us instinctively to reach up (or in), seeking to connect with the Higher Realm, the Muse, the soul, the neshama.

Meanwhile the Higher Realm is reaching down, trying to help us, seeking to open and widen the channels of communication. There's only one problem:

Between the two levels is that negative force that I call Resistance.

They didn't teach you about Resistance in school. They didn't teach me. I became aware of its existence, like every other writer and artist, by having it kick my ass for seven straight years and nearly kill me.

Resistance, as we all know, is the force—the dark force—whose job is to keep us from connecting with the soul, and to keep the soul from connecting with us.

In artistic terms, Resistance's job is to keep us from writing our novel, composing our symphony, initiating our startup.

In Jewish mysticism, this force is called the *yetzer hara*. Google it.

Resistance is the dragon that guards the gold—the gold of our authentic self, our true voice, our artistic and personal destiny.

"ETERNITY IS IN LOVE WITH THE CREATIONS OF TIME"

This quote comes from the great English mystical poet, William Blake. I cited it in *The War of Art*, page 116.

What Blake meant, I think, is that the higher dimension is invested emotionally in, and participates actively in the material plane. He was confirming what the Kabbalists believed: that the neshama is constantly striving to communicate with us and aid us down here on the physical plane.

This force—this active, positive, invisible, indestructible, ever-evolving, inextinguishable creative force—is the equal-and-opposite reaction to the negative force of Resistance... and the power behind every artist and every artistic creation.

THE UNCONSCIOUS AND
THE DIVINE GROUND

Also in *The War of Art*, I related a story about a seminar I attended once, taught by Tom Laughlin ("Billy Jack"), who in his non-cinematic life was a well-known, if controversial, Jungian teacher and counselor. Tom Laughlin drew this schematic of the human psyche.

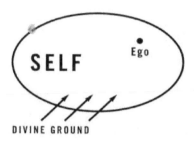

I had no idea what Tom meant by "the Divine Ground" but the phrase struck me like a two-by-four, particularly the notion that our own limited minds lie psychologically adjacent to it and in fact *touching it*.

I believed it at once.

Why not?

Mystics of all cultures have subscribed to this notion. They've in fact based their entire lives and philosophies upon it. To them, consciousness is not only not limited to the individual's physical body, it's not limited to the individual's lifetime.

Hey, I'm with them!

I can't prove it (who can?) but I swear there's a part of our psyche that butts up against Something that's infinitely greater, wiser, and more powerful, and that Something is conscious, universal, intelligent, active, collective, possibly infinite.

I'll go further. I believe that that Something transcends time and space. It knows past and future, up and down, in and out, backhand and forehand.

THE CONSCIOUS MIND
AND THE HIGHER REALM

Two more ideas that can't be proven:

1. This greater mind can be accessed by our lesser minds.

(Of course this is true; artists do it every day. So do you and I in our dreams.)

The artist's stock-in-trade, as we said, is the ability to shuttle back and forth between Level #1 and Level #2, in other words between the conscious mind and the Higher Realm.

2. This greater mind *wants* to be accessed. It is actively reaching out to us, seeking our attention and participation.

> ... the mystics, the gnostics, adherents of the grail and alchemists [writes John P. Dourley in *Jung and his Mystics*] All these traditions share the sense that mind is natively imbued with the latent awareness of its universal connectedness. The development of this awareness intensifies the sense

of the divine. This reconnection of
the mind with its divine ground happens pre-eminently through the
work of the dream and its symbols,
expressing the energy of the divine.

All art arises from this divine ground, whether the artist is aware of it or not (or even actively denies it).

But why, you ask.

Even if there is such a thing as the Divine Ground, Level #2, the Higher Realm, why would it care about the fate or affairs of humankind? Are we suggesting that it actively participates in human affairs?

Really?

Toward what end?

THE ARTIST'S VOCATION

All art—dance, drama, architecture, literature, music, etc.—is about the recognition of beauty and the articulation of empathy and compassion for the Other.

The artist is a force for unity. Her role is to bring together, upon the common ground of the imagination, the disparate and often warring factions of the mortal psyche and the human race.

The artist does this not en masse but one-on-one, individual by individual. She performs this alchemy within the human heart, which she enters by the medium of the imagination.

A documentary about sable hunters in Siberia or a film about a family in Tehran dealing with Alzheimer's transports the foreign viewer, like you and me, into a universe whose existence we had never known and makes that world and those who inhabit it immediate and vivid and human. No longer can we say or think, "These people are not like me."

We see that they are.

The gulf of separation has been bridged, at least for the moment, by one tiny increment. What has replaced it is the power of empathy, of compassion, of identification with the Other.

The artist does that.

A work of art is a unifying force. Great art transcends divisions of culture, race, nationality, history. It vanquishes time itself. The cave paintings at Lascaux are as powerful today as they were seventeen thousand years ago, just as the grace and symmetry of the Golden Gate Bridge could be appreciated by the most "primitive" hunter-gatherer.

THE HERO'S JOURNEY OF
THE HUMAN RACE

If the individual has a hero's journey, does the race collectively possess one as well?

If it does, what is our communal "call"?

What "threshold" do we as a race seek to cross?

What "home" will we return to?

What "gift" shall we bring?

Here's what I think:

I think the race's journey began in the Garden of Eden (which is of course a myth, but a myth common in one form or another to all humanity.)

Our inciting incident was a crime, the eating of the fruit of the Tree of Knowledge.

Act One ended with the Almighty casting us out of the garden.

We entered the Inverted World then, humankind's collective Act Two, and we've been there ever since, suffering trials, undergoing initiations, encountering creatures of wonder, while our hearts, as Homer wrote of Odysseus:

> ...through all the seafaring, ached with an agony
> to redeem [ourselves] and bring [our] company
> safe home.

Safe home to the Garden—that's the return we seek. That alone will complete the circle and make mankind whole.

The artist is the herald and the medium of this passage.

BECAUSE THE ARTIST
SHUTTLES BETWEEN WORLDS

The artist's skill, we have said, is to shuttle between the conscious mind and the higher mind, the Divine Ground.

That's her job.

It's what she does every day.

For "conscious mind" read the alienation and exile of the human condition.

For "divine ground" read lost paradise, the Garden of Eden.

It is not an overstatement, I believe, to declare that the artist's role is to lead the human race back to Eden.

True, artists don't know this. They don't get up each morning with this enterprise in mind. In fact if you articulated this to them, they'd probably laugh in your face.

But they are the heralds and mentors of mankind's hero's journey nonetheless. Their charge is, as James Joyce phrased it in *Portrait of the Artist as a Young Man*:

> ...to forge in the smithy of my soul the uncreated conscience of the race.

How do artists perform this service? By producing works whose fruit, for the reader or viewer, is empathy and compassion for the Other and, ultimately, identification with the Other.

The track that artists shuttle upon each day between the conventional world and the world of the higher mind is the same trolley line that the human race as a whole is seeking to board—the track from the narrow, fearful, divisive ego to the open, loving, inclusive Self.

THE ARTIST AND THE GARDEN

The artist's role is to complete the circle that started with Adam and Eve. Her charge is to lead us back to Eden, not in the state of unconsciousness and dependence in which we stood before the Fall, but in full awareness of ourselves and our station, our mortality, and of the greater world around and within us.

The artist's role is to make the unconscious conscious.

She may not realize this. She may be blind to it. She may perform this task by instinct, not design. But she performs it just the same.

She is compelled by her nature.

She may work her entire life and never even realize she is doing this. But she is.

The Fall created the "multiplicity of forms" and dissevered the race from unity with the Divine Ground. The artist's role is to shatter the illusion of separation and isolation and to blaze the trail back to the condition of Oneness, which state has always been mankind's true condition but which we as individuals have been blinded to, immured as we are within the prison of our separate egos.

AN ORIGINAL CRIME
(BUT A GREAT AND NOBLE ONE)

Christians believe in Original Sin. Jews cite in Genesis 6:5 and 8:21, the appearance within the human heart of the *yetzer hara*, "a turning toward evil." The ancient Greeks as well believed in a primal crime, which prompted the hero's journey, as Homer declares of Odysseus ...

> ... who, after he had plundered the innermost citadel of hallowed Troy, was made to stray grievously about the coasts of men ...

When we speak of the Call that initiates the hero's journey, it's often an opportunity that suddenly appears, an imposed expulsion, an emergency that demands action. But not infrequently it's a crime—a wrong committed, usually in ignorance or unconsciousness, by the hero. In the case above, Odysseus violates the sacred precinct of the goddess. In the Garden, Adam and Eve eat of the fruit of the tree of knowledge.

A crime causes both protagonists to be "cast out."

The human race's crime is identifying with the ego. It's Adam and Eve's original sin—and Odysseus's and yours and mine.

But give our forebears some credit. Their crime was a great and noble one, a step toward divinity, a reaching for the stars.

THE FALL OF MAN

The following is from Aldous Huxley, *The Perennial Philosophy*:

> In the Hebrew-Christian tradition the Fall is
> subsequent to creation and is due exclusively
> to the egocentric use of a free will, which
> ought to have remained centred in the divine
> Ground and not in the separate selfhood. The
> myth of Genesis ... to be adequate to our expe-
> rience ... would have to be modified ... it would
> have to make clear that creation, the incom-
> prehensible passage from the unmanifested
> One into the manifest multiplicity of nature,
> from eternity into time, is not merely the pre-
> lude and necessary condition of the Fall; to
> some extent it is the Fall.
>
> That the passage from the unity of spiri-
> tual to the manifoldness of temporal being is
> an essential part of the Fall is clearly stated in
> the Buddhist and Hindu renderings of the
> Perennial Philosophy. Pain and evil are in-
> separable from human existence in a world
> of time; and, for human beings, there is an
> intensification of this inevitable pain and evil

when the desire is turned towards the self and the many, rather than toward the divine Ground.

And this from *Beyond Psyche: Symbol and Transcendence in C. G. Jung* by Mark R. Gundry:

> ... I find two fundamental movements that pull conscious awareness beyond its normal horizon. The *first movement* begins with the suspension of directed thinking and the consequent activation of the symbol-producing function. The symbol mysteriously arises through the play of dreaming and active imagination, mediates unconscious depth to our awareness, and infuses life with differentiated affect. This process creates an opportunity to recognize that a whole range of psychic activity is at work apart from the ego's normal functioning. Such recognition pulls us beyond our usual horizon of awareness. We know ourselves not simply as the "I" of intentional acts, but as a psyche whose reality extends far beyond the "I."

This is some deep shit, isn't it? I confess I don't understand half of it.

THE FALL OF MAN, PART TWO

Here's my shot at grasping the stuff from the preceding chapter, *from the point of view of the artist.*

Garden of Eden. The serpent tempts Adam and Eve to eat of the fruit of the Tree of Knowledge. They do.

Holy shit! Suddenly the primeval pair realize they are individuals, human beings, separate from nature. They are not like the eagle or the lion, who are always and at all times in perfect union with their essence, the Divine Ground, i.e., the all-inclusive consciousness they possessed before they bit into that fruit.

[Trivia note: nowhere does Genesis say it was an apple.]

This is the Fall.

God kicks Adam and Eve out of the garden. He banishes them from union with the Divine Ground.

If indeed you and I are descended from this First Couple, our human state of mind, the intuitive sense that we all share of being fallen from Paradise, is the natural result of their—Adam and Eve's—original crime.

Since that day we've all been trying to get back to Eden.

The mystic does it by altering his consciousness through meditation, prayer, asceticism, renunciation of the senses, the ingestion of mind-altering substances.

The lover does it by seeking sublime union with another.

The mother does it in her way, the warrior in his, the philosopher in a third manner. Even the suicide bomber treads this same path.

What about the artist?

What about you and me?

We trek this same highway. We too are seeking to get back to the Garden, to reconnect to the Divine Ground. How do we do it?

Through our work.

Or, more accurately, through *the act by which we pursue our work*.

When Bob Dylan writes a song, when Twyla Tharp choreographs a dance, when Parker and Stone write a new episode of *South Park*, they shift their consciousness out of N for Normal and into S for Superconscious, that is:

> ...the suspension of directed thinking and the consequent activation of the symbol-producing function. The symbol mysteriously arises through the play of dreaming and active imagination, [producing] a whole range of psychic activity ... apart from the ego's normal functioning. Such recognition [enables us to] know ourselves not simply as the "I" of intentional acts, but as a psyche whose reality extends far beyond the "I."

This is the Times Square to Grand Central shuttle we spoke of earlier. The artist toggles her platform of effort between the conscious and the unconscious, between the rational mind and the Divine Ground.

This is also the rush of working as an artist. This is what makes the process addictive.

THE SOUL'S CODE

Have you read *The Soul's Code* by James Hillman? I highly recommend it.

In *The Soul's Code*, Mr. Hillman introduces the concept of the *daimon*. Daimon is a Greek word. The equivalent term in Latin is *genius*.

Both words refer to an inhering spirit. We are born, each of us, (says James Hillman) with our own individual daimon. The daimon is our guardian. It knows our destiny. It kens our calling.

James Hillman makes an analogy to an acorn. The totality of the full-grown oak is contained—every leaf and every branch—already within the acorn.

THE DAIMON IN ACTION

My friend Hermes Melissanidis won the gold medal at the '96 Atlanta Olympics in the floor exercise of men's gymnastics. Here's a story of his daimon.

When Hermes was eight, he saw gymnastics for the first time on TV. He knew instantly that this was what he wanted to do. He went to his parents and asked them to arrange for a trainer so he could study gymnastics and compete for Greece on the Olympic team.

Hermes' family is a family of doctors. His mom is a doctor. His dad is a doctor. They're all doctors in Hermes' family. They were horrified when they heard their son's passionate conviction that he wanted to be a gymnast. "Absolutely not!" The family would never condone Hermes wasting his youth on this preposterous endeavor.

Hermes went on a hunger strike.

For four days he ate nothing.

Finally his distraught parents agreed to discuss the issue. The family and eight-year-old Hermes came to a compromise. Hermes would be allowed to study gymnastics full time. His parents would arrange it and pay for it. But Hermes must promise that he would also become a doctor. He agreed. And in fact he did graduate from medical school along with becoming an Olympic gold medalist. Today he's an actor, by the way.

Do you see Hermes' daimon in this story? The daimon knew Hermes' gymnastic destiny. It seized him. It compelled him to act. Why else would an eight-year-old go on a hunger strike? The daimon knew.

We could easily cite a thousand other such stories—Eleanor Roosevelt, Jackson Pollock, Colette, Hemingway, on and on—of individuals whose sense of their own destiny was so strong in them that nothing including their own fear and self-doubt and even their common sense could stop them from living it out.

DO YOU HAVE A DAIMON?

It took me nineteen years to earn my first dollar as a pure creative writer and twenty-eight years to get my first novel published.

I had jobs in advertising. I had work in other fields. I always quit to write. Bosses, with the best of intentions, would call me into their offices and urge me to listen to reason: stay here, you've got a future with us, don't throw your life away on a dream that's never going to come true.

Every time I would agonize. Am I crazy? How can I go off again to write another novel that nobody will want to read and that no publishing house will want to publish?

But I always left the job. I always went off to write.

That's the daimon.

MY HERO, JAMES RHODES

Here's a passage from an article in the *Guardian UK* by James Rhodes, the concert pianist.

> I didn't play the piano for 10 years. A decade of slow death by greed working in the City, chasing something that never existed in the first place [security, self-worth, etc.] And only when the pain of not doing it got greater than the imagined pain of doing it did I somehow find the balls to pursue what I really wanted and had been obsessed by since the age of seven—to be a concert pianist.

> Admittedly I went a little extreme—no income for five years, six hours a day of intense practice, monthly four-day long lessons with a brilliant and psychopathic teacher in Verona, a hunger for something that was so necessary it cost me my marriage, nine months in a mental hospital, most of my dignity and about 35lbs in weight. And the pot of gold at the end of the rainbow is not perhaps the Disney ending I'd envisaged as I lay in bed aged 10 listening to Horowitz devouring Rachmaninov at Carnegie Hall.

My life involves endless hours of repetitive and frustrating practising, lonely hotel rooms, dodgy pianos, aggressively bitchy reviews, isolation, confusing airline reward programmes, physiotherapy, stretches of nervous boredom (counting ceiling tiles backstage as the house slowly fills up) punctuated by short moments of extreme pressure (playing 120,000 notes from memory in the right order with the right fingers, the right sound, the right pedalling while chatting about the composers and pieces and knowing there are critics, recording devices, my mum, the ghosts of the past, all there watching), and perhaps most crushingly, the realisation that I will never, ever give the perfect recital. It can only ever, with luck, hard work and a hefty dose of self-forgiveness, be "good enough."

And yet. The indescribable reward of taking a bunch of ink on paper from the shelf at Chappell of Bond Street. Tubing it home, setting the score, pencil, coffee and ashtray on the piano and emerging a few days, weeks or months later able to perform something that some mad, genius, lunatic of a composer 300 years ago heard in his head while out of his mind with grief or love or syphilis. A piece of music that will always baffle the greatest minds in the world, that simply cannot be made sense of, that is still living and floating in the ether and will do so for yet more centuries to come. That is extraordinary. And I did that. I do it, to my continual astonishment, all the time.

That's the daimon. There's a reason why our English word *demon* comes so close to it.

You have to be a little crazy. Maybe more than a little.

THE PAIN OF NOT DOING IT

The key sentence in James Rhodes' article, to me, is this:

> ... only when the pain of not doing it got greater than the imagined pain of doing it did I somehow find the balls to pursue what I really wanted and had been obsessed by since the age of seven—to be a concert pianist.

That pain is the pain of the daimon, imprisoned in its owner's body and prevented by its owner's fear from stepping forth and living out its destiny. When James Rhodes plunged into his "piano course," he set his daimon free. He followed it. He surrendered to it.

That's how the daimon expresses itself. It inflicts such inner torment on us that it compels us to respond to its demands.

PAIN AND THE ARTIST

It's a commonplace that artists work to free themselves from pain. The irritation of the grain of sand compels the oyster to produce a pearl.

But what is the *real* pain beneath any personal anguish that you or I may feel or have suffered?

It is the pain of being mortal and being aware of our mortality, of being an isolated individual in a world seemingly devoid of meaning. In other words, the pain of getting kicked out of the Garden.

> Pain and evil are inseparable from human existence in a world of time; and, for human beings, there is an intensification of this inevitable pain and evil when the desire is turned toward the self and the many, rather than toward the Divine Ground.

To access the Divine Ground—in other words, to write, to compose, to shoot film—plugs us in, for this hour at least, to the garden we were expelled from. For a few moments we get to breathe again that Edenic air, to experience that primal fragrance.

And better than that, we get to point our brothers and sisters toward it.

A great song.
An unforgettable image.
A sublime story.
We need it.
It stops the pain.

AUTOBIOGRAPHY OF THE DAIMON

What follows is founded upon no science. I can cite no studies; I have no evidence. These suppositions are purely idiosyncratic, based only on my own experience:

1.   The daimon is immortal.

I can't prove it. I just feel it. When you and I shuffle off this mortal coil, our daimons will step down to the shoulder of the highway as lightly as a hitchhiker being left off at the end of a ride. Our daimon will trot off into the underbrush, like the Bengal tiger in *Life of Pi*, without a backward glance. It will pick up the next iteration of "you" and "me" and move on.

2.   The daimon is divine.

The daimon arises from and dwells upon a level beyond the material. It is governed not by the laws of the physical plane, but by the precepts of heaven.

3.   The daimon is inhuman.

Mother Teresa had a daimon. Martin Luther King had one. But so did Hitler. So did Stalin. And so do you.

There's a reason why *daimon* looks a lot like *demon*. The concepts of right and wrong are foreign to the daimon. The daimon operates by higher laws. The daimon is nature. An oak will grow through solid concrete. A butterfly will cross hundreds of miles of open ocean.

4. The daimon is monstrous.

The human race lost something, I believe, when it passed from the ancient world to the modern. The ancients understood the monstrous. They were not appalled by it, as we are. The legends of the ancient world are packed with monsters— Medusa, Cerberus, the Minotaur. Even the human characters— Medea, Agamemnon, Ajax, Clytemnestra—often embody the monstrous.

The ancients recognized that nature herself contains the monstrous. The world as the Almighty designed it is populated by monsters.

5. The daimon is creative.

The daimon's role is to carry the new. It is the Big Bang. It bears the future.

6. Your daimon is closer to you than anything or anyone in your life.

Your daimon shields you, protects you, counsels you. It kicks your ass. It will drive you crazy if you ignore it, and yet it is inseparable from you. Nothing in your life is as loyal. It will never leave you, never betray you, never abandon you.

No creature of humankind—not your spouse, your mother, your sainted aunt—understands you like your daimon.

You will never understand yourself to the depth that your daimon understands you.

7. You are not your daimon.

And yet you are not your daimon, and your daimon is not you. You are the vessel for your daimon. You are the latest edition in a long line. You are the raw material with which the daimon works.

8. Ignore the daimon and it will kill you.

Are we nobler than our daimons? Are we "kinder"? "Better"? Perhaps. But our daimon is far more powerful.

9. The meaning of your life is contained in your daimon.

THE ARTIST SERVES NECESSITY

Let's return to our Model of the Universe, the Artist's Universe. Does it coincide in any way with the hero's journey?

Could this model of the universe also be a template that has existed from birth within our psyches?

Consider:

1. You, the artist, are the hero.
2. Resistance is the villain.
3. The call comes from your daimon.
4. The journey is your life as an artist—the works you will produce over your lifetime.
5. The neshama (your soul, your Self) is the source of the aid you receive on this journey. This assistance comes from mentors, from boon companions, from spirit animals, from lovers, from old crones, even from enemies. It comes from the unconscious/superconscious, from that part of our psyches that touches upon the divine.
6. The neshama acts in the service of an entity that we have not yet spoken of.

The ancients called this entity Necessity.

Necessity is the oldest of the gods and the one before whom all others bow.

What is Necessity? It is the future. It is That Which Is Not Yet, But Which Will Be.

No force in the universe can stand against Necessity.

You, the artist, serve Necessity. That is the call you receive from your daimon, to do your part, even though you have no conception of the greater whole or the Greater Drama.

BRINGING IT ALL BACK HOME

All this sounds very occult and mysto, doesn't it?

What do we do with this in the real world? Here on planet Earth, we're just trying to write a freakin' short story and maybe sell it to somebody! How do we do it?

How do we overcome our own self-doubt and self-sabotage, our fear of success and fear of failure, our tendency to procrastination, to perfectionism, to yield to distraction, temptation, confusion, etc. All the symptoms and manifestations of Resistance?

"Steve," you say, "I don't feel like a hero. I don't have a Call. I don't have a spirit raccoon. I can barely find my way down to the subway, let alone into some mysterious dimension of creativity or the future. Please tell me: how do I find my life's work, if in fact I even have such a crazy thing? And what do I do with it once I've found it?"

PUT YOUR ASS WHERE YOUR HEART WANTS TO BE

The great secret that every artist and mystic knows is that the profound can be reached best by concentrating upon the mundane.

Do you want to write? Sit down at the keyboard.

Wanna paint? Stand before an easel.

Wanna dance? Get your butt into the studio.

Want the goddess to show up for you? Show up for her.

THE CREATIVE HABIT

I begin each day of my life with a ritual.

This is the renowned choreographer Twyla Tharp from her indispensable book, *The Creative Habit*.

> I wake up at 5:30 a.m., put on my workout clothes, my leg warmers, my sweatshirts, and my hat. I walk outside my Manhattan home, hail a taxi, and the tell the driver to take me to the Pumping Iron gym at 91st Street and First Avenue, where I work out for two hours. The ritual is not the stretching and the weight training I put my body through each morning at the gym; the ritual is the cab. The moment I tell the driver where to go I have completed the ritual.

Ms. Tharp goes on.

> It's a simple act, but doing it the same way each morning habitualizes it—makes it repeatable, easy to do. It reduces the chance that I would skip it or do it differently. It is one

more item in my arsenal of routines, and one
less thing to think about.

The timeless truth that Ms. Tharp is articulating here is
this:

That the mysterious "flow" of creativity can be primed like
a pump by physically (and emotionally) planting yourself in
the physical space where you want that energy to flow.

ART IS WORK

And unto Adam He said, "Because thou hast hearkened to the voice of thy wife, and hast eaten of the tree, of which I have commanded you, saying Thou shalt not eat of it; cursed is the ground for thy sake; in sorrow shalt thou eat of it all the days of thy life; Thorns also and thistles shall it bring forth for thee; and thou shalt eat the herb of the field; in the sweat of thy face shalt thou eat bread, till thou return unto the ground; for out of it wast thou taken: for dust thou art, and unto dust shalt thou return." And Adam called his wife's name Eve; because she was the mother of all living.

The artist's role, whether she understands it or not, is to point the way back to the Garden, to that state of consciousness that the human race enjoyed before the Fall. In other words, to direct contact with, and experience of, the Divine Ground.

But note the Almighty's curse, as He kicked the mom and dad of our race out of paradise.

The way back, if indeed it is through art, comes via a ticket paid for in sweat.

Art is work.

WHO YOU ARE IS WHAT YOU WRITE

The artist discovers herself *by the work she produces.*

Who are you?

Dance and find out.

Sing and find out.

Write and find out.

> Writing, like life itself, [Henry Miller again] is a voyage of discovery. The adventure is a metaphysical one: it is a way of approaching life indirectly, of acquiring a total rather than a partial view of the universe. The writer lives between the upper and lower worlds: he takes the path in order eventually to become that path himself ...
>
> From the very beginning almost I was deeply aware that there is no goal. I never hope to embrace the whole, but merely to give in each separate fragment, each work, the feeling of the whole as I go on, because I am digging deeper and deeper into life, digging deeper and deeper into past and future. With the endless burrowing a certitude develops which is greater than faith or belief. I become

more and more indifferent to my fate, as writer, and more and more certain of my destiny as a man.

There is a dimension of reality above (or below) the material dimension we live in.

If you're an artist, the search for that dimension is your life.

"THE BENIGN, PROTECTING POWER OF DESTINY"

Do you believe we're not alone on our journey? Do you subscribe to the notion, as I do, that help appears from sources we can neither name nor explain?

Here's Joseph Campbell from *The Hero with a Thousand Faces*:

> For those who have not refused the call, the first encounter of the [hero's] journey is with a protective figure ... who provides the adventurer with amulets against the dragon forces he is about to pass. What such a figure represents is the benign, protecting power of destiny. The fantasy is a reassurance—promise that the peace of Paradise ... is not to be lost; that it supports the present and stands in the future as well as in the past ... [that] protective power is always and ever present within or just behind the unfamiliar features of the world. One has only to know and trust, and the ageless guardians will appear. Having responded to his own call, and continuing to follow courageously as the consequences unfold, the hero finds all the forces of the unconscious at his side. Mother

Nature herself supports the mighty task. And in so far as the hero's act coincides with that for which his society is ready, he seems to ride on the great rhythm of the historical process.

In other words, the artist and the hero are working individually and collectively on a "mighty task" supported by Nature and protected by forces, not only of the unconscious, but of the real world, in real time.

HOW I WORK

Before I sit down at the keyboard each day, I stand and say a prayer to the Muse. I say it out loud, in absolute earnest.

Why do I do this?

Because when I enter my office, I cross the threshold into a different dimension, a sacred dimension. I'm not being fatuous or facetious when I say this.

I have no idea what I will write that day. I have an intention. I have an object. But I don't know what will appear from one sentence to the next.

I need help. I need the participation and the aid of forces from that different plane of reality. I don't know what to name these forces so I call them "the Muse." It's a concept that's congenial to me. I like it. I can relate to it.

Maybe that realm is the unconscious, the superconscious. Maybe, as Jung suggests, that part of the psyche lies adjacent to the Divine Ground, in other words to some higher realm of consciousness, of being, in which, I hope and assume, death does not hold sway, nor time or space, and no individual is separated emotionally or spiritually from any other. In this dimension, I'd like to believe, the future already exists. It is known or can be known.

Can any of this be true?

I don't know.

But I act as if it were.

To me it is true.

This is the world I live in.

So I invoke the Muse. I subordinate myself to the goddess. I seek her aid. I place myself before her in the posture of a soldier, a servant, a supplicant.

When I sit down to work, I draw the bowstring the same way Eugen Herrigel did and, like him, my object is to let the string release itself without my conscious participation.

It took me thirty years to learn how to do this. That time, or the greater part of it, was my artist's journey, an adventure that continues to this day.

And you know what? It works.

I have said many times that the Muse is the only female to whom I have always been faithful. This is true.

And she has always been true to me.

THE ARTIST'S JOURNEY IS THE HERO'S JOURNEY OF THE HUMAN RACE

You may wonder as you sit in your cubicle designing a gun-down scene for *Call of Duty Black Ops IV* if you're really advancing the cause of humanity.

You are.

Your artist's journey is unique to you. You alone are on your path. Your job is only to follow it and be true to it.

Who knows what heights it may eventually bear you to?

You are an artist. Your journey—however humble, however fraught, however beset with thorns and thistles—is part of a noble, cosmic cause. It is not meaningless. It is not in vain.

It is a portion of a grand adventure.

The artist's journey is the hero's journey of the human race.

THE GREAT ADVENTURE

What is "the benign, protecting power of destiny," if indeed there is such a thing?

I think it's the evolutionary pull of all humankind, which seeks, like the hero, to return to the start of its journey—in other words, the great-circle trajectory of the race arcing home to Eden.

If mankind is indeed on a collective hero's journey, then Creation itself is on our side.

The Ego is the enemy.

Resistance is the force that it uses against us.

These foes are mighty indeed. But opposed to them always, and equal if not greater, are the forces of the daimon, the neshama, the Divine Ground, and the great-circle "destiny," to use Joseph Campbell's word. That is the wind at our backs.

Therefore, be of good cheer, brothers and sisters.

A powerful destiny lies coiled inside you. This force is neither a dumb, robotic tape or some dusty hieroglyph left from millions of years ago, but an active, dynamic, intelligent presence—endlessly creative, ever-mutating, responsive-in-the-moment—supporting and guiding you as you evolve and advance.

Nor does this force operate only inside your mind. It is not solely cerebral or abstract, nor is it bound by the limits of your consciousness or your physical body.

It operates in real time and in the real world. It is connected to forces unconstrained by time and space, by reason or by nature's laws. It is capable of summoning allies and assistance and of concentrating them on your behalf and in your cause. These forces are not only of the imagination—ideas, insights, wisdom, breakthroughs in your life and work—but also practical and material apparitions like friends and allies, connections, places to stay, money.

Flesh-and-blood individuals will enter your life at precisely the time and place you need them. These persons will play the role of archetypes—mentors and lovers, boon companions, even animal spirits, tricksters—as will corresponding foes and antagonists, tempters and temptresses, enemies, shape-shifters.

The hero's journey and the artist's journey are real. They come with the promise of change, of passion, of fulfillment and of self-actualization, and they come with the curse of Eden—"henceforth shalt thou eat thy bread in the sweat of thy face"—which mandates unrelenting toil and labor. The struggle never ends. It never gets easier.

This is what you were born for.

Nature has built you for this.

The artist is a role ordained by Creation. Even if you know nothing of this mandate, or refuse to believe it, or have forgotten it entirely, even if you flat-out reject it, this living force remains vital and irresistible inside you. You cannot run from it. You cannot stand against it. It is more alive inside you than your own blood and more impossible to resist than the urge to survive or to procreate or to find love.

A great adventure awaits you.

Ready or not, you are called.

HOW DO YOU KNOW?

The answer is: You decide.

You decide, and you prove your decision by action.

You write.

You paint.

You shoot film.

You start and you keep going.

Does this sound hard core, even cruel? It's not me talking. It's the goddess.

When she looks down on you from the Next Level, deciding whether she will gift you with her blessings, she is scrutinizing you the way Steve Jobs would look at an applicant for a top-secret project at Apple or the way the Navy SEALs would regard a candidate who says, "Sign me up, I wanna fight."

Life or death.

In or out.

Do it or don't do it.

A BODY OF WORK

In the Hindu religion there's a concept called "being a house-holder."

A householder is one who practices his or her religion, not apart like a monk in a cloister, but in the real world. Raising a family. Practicing a profession. Engaged actively in the community.

In India, the calling of a householder is thought of as higher than that of an ascetic or a renunciant because it's harder. It requires greater strength of mind and dedication of will.

You can do that as an artist. Nothing can stop you.

You can practice your art. You can produce, over time, a body of work that is the produce of your calling, the fruit of your authentic being, the full expression of your truest and highest self.

SPECIAL THANKS

My deepest gratitude to David Mamet, Rosanne Cash, Twyla Tharp, James Rhodes and every other man, woman and elemental source of insight whom I have quoted, cited or excerpted in these pages—Joseph Campbell, C.G. Jung, the King James Bible, Socrates slash Plato, the Buddha, James Hillman, Christopher Vogler, Blake Snyder, Mark R. Gundry, Aldous Huxley, Homer, James Joyce, John P. Dourley, Tom Laughlin, Eugen Herrigel, Bob Dylan, Joni Mitchell, Philip Roth, Martin Scorsese, the Rolling Stones, Bruce Springsteen, Hermes Melissanidis, Meryl Streep, William Blake and the ubiquitous Henry Miller.

And to Shawn and Kate and Callie, without whom, etc.

Thanks, you guys!

CPSIA information can be obtained
at www.ICGtesting.com
Printed in the USA
LVHW111159301018
595341LV00001B/153/P

9 781936 891542